THE STORY OF THE
NEW JERSEY
NETS

CREATIVE EDUCATION

Published by Creative Education
123 South Broad Street
Mankato, Minnesota 56001
Creative Education is an imprint of The Creative Company.

DESIGN AND PRODUCTION BY **EVANSDAY DESIGN**

PHOTOGRAPHS BY Getty Images (Ray Amati / NBAE, Nathaniel S.
Butler / NBAE, Jim Cummins / NBAE, Melissa Farlow / National
Geographic, Focus on Sport, Jesse D. Garrabrant / NBAE, Andy
Hayt, Walter Looss Jr. / NBAE, Ron Koch / NBAE, Jim McIsaac,
Fernando Medina / NBAE, NBAE, NBA Photo Library / NBAE,
Anthony Nest, Ed Pagliariini–Pool, Mike Powell, Amy
Toensing, Noren Trotman / NBAE)

LIBRARY OF CONGRESS CATALOGING-IN-PUBLICATION DATA

LeBoutillier, Nate.
The story of the New Jersey Nets / by Nate LeBoutillier.
p. cm. — (The NBA—a history of hoops)
Includes index.
ISBN-13: 978-1-58341-416-3
1. New Jersey Nets (Basketball team)—History—
Juvenile literature. I. Title. II. Series.

GV885.52.N37L43 2006
796.323'64'0974941—dc22   2005051775

First edition

9 8 7 6 5 4 3 2 1

COVER PHOTO: *Vince Carter*

THE STORY OF THE
NEW JERSEY
NETS

NATE LeBOUTILLIER

CREATIVE C EDUCATION

BASKETBALL MAKES A KALEIDOSCOPE OF COLORS AS IT BOUNCES ALONG, THE SAME COLORS AS THE NEW JERSEY NETS' UNIFORMS. ONE PLAYER, JULIUS "DR. J" ERVING, BREAKS FROM THE PACK TO GRAB IT. THE BALL LOOKS LIKE A GRAPEFRUIT IN HIS LARGE HAND AS HE DRIBBLES, DASHING TOWARD THE RIM. ALL AT ONCE HE TAKES OFF—HIS LONG LIMBS FLOATING TOWARD THE RIM. THE MOMENTUM BLOWS BACK HIS LARGE AFRO, AND HE EXTENDS THE BALL LIKE A TORCH, LOOKING LIKE SOME SPORTS VERSION OF THE STATUE OF LIBERTY.

THE DOCTOR HAS MADE ANOTHER HOUSE CALL.

NEW JERSEY NETS
East Rutherford New Jersey

THE NETS COME TO BE

NEW JERSEY IS A STATE Of GREAT VARIETY. WITH ITS northern tip near New York City and its southern tip near Philadelphia, much of the state is comprised of urban and suburban communities. Yet the state is also famous for its scenic farming regions, which have inspired its nickname—the "Garden State."

Up until the late 1960s, basketball fans in New Jersey split their allegiance. Some rooted for the Knicks in New York, and others cheered for the Warriors and then the 76ers in Philadelphia. Finally, in 1967, New Jersey got a franchise of its own in the American Basketball Association (ABA) and named it the "Americans."

9

One of the greatest pure shooters the NBA has ever seen, Rick Barry emerged as the Nets' first star

Center Billy Paultz averaged more than 14 points and 10 rebounds a game in his first four Nets seasons

When the ABA was formed in February 1967, the league had high hopes but not much cash. That meant that ABA teams often played in low-rent arenas and featured second-level talent compared to the National Basketball Association (NBA). The New Jersey Americans were one of the original members of the ABA. The Americans played their home games in Teaneck, New Jersey, in a gloomy U.S. military building. The building's roof leaked, and one home game even had to be postponed because of rain. The Americans finished their first season 36–42.

The next season, the Americans relocated to New York's Long Island and became known as the New York Nets. The Nets suffered through a disappointing 17–61 season that year, and fewer than 1,000 people showed up to see most of the club's home games. In 1969, a wealthy businessman named Roy Boe bought the team. In 1970, former NBA scoring champ Rick Barry joined the team. "I think Rick Barry is the greatest and most productive offensive forward ever to play the game," said Bill Sharman, Barry's former coach with the San Francisco Warriors.

Barry, center Billy "The Whopper" Paultz, guard Johnny Roche, and forward Trooper Washington helped the Nets post a winning record for the first time in 1971–72. The club even reached the final round of the ABA playoffs that year before losing the championship to the Indiana Pacers.

PAGING DR. J

IN 1972, A JUDGE RULED THAT BARRY HAD TO RETURN to his old NBA club, the Golden State Warriors. But the next year, Roy Boe made up for the loss by trading for superstar Julius Erving, giving the Nets one of the ABA's most spectacular scorers. Erving was nicknamed "Dr. J" for the way he "operated" on the court. The 6-foot-6 forward moved with astonishing speed and grace, and his soaring dunks filled sports highlight films. "Doc goes up and never comes down," said Nets guard Bill Melchionni.

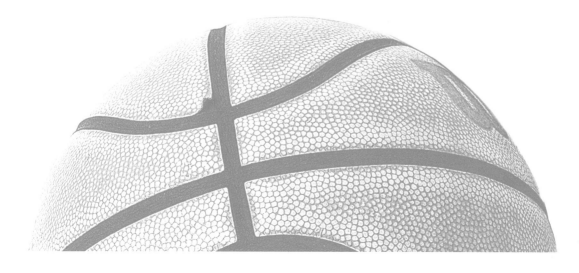

13

Julius Erving earned fame as the most graceful and creative shot-maker in all of basketball in the 1970s

14

Some fans called guard John Williamson "Super John" for his ability to score a lot of points in a hurry

The Nets didn't come down either during the 1973–74 season, Dr. J's first with the club. They won 55 regular-season games, 25 more than the previous year. To top off the year, the Nets routed the Utah Stars in the league finals to win their first ABA championship, and Dr. J earned his own title— ABA Most Valuable Player (MVP).

Two seasons later, the Nets staged a virtual replay of that magical year. They duplicated their 55–29 record, Dr. J again led the league in scoring with an average of 29 points per game, and New York romped to its second ABA championship.

That 1975–76 season marked the end of the ABA's brief history. The ABA and NBA merged in early 1976, and four ABA franchises, including the Nets, joined the bigger and older league. But Erving was involved in a contract dispute with Boe, who refused to pay his star more money. In the end, Boe sold Dr. J's contract to the Philadelphia 76ers. "How could anyone do this to us?" wondered Nets guard John Williamson. "Our season is over already." Williamson turned out to be right. Without the Doctor, the 1976–77 Nets plummeted to an NBA-worst 22–60 record.

THE DOCTOR DEPARTS

In 1976, New York basketball fans found this advertisement in their local newspapers: *See the fantastic Dr. "J" in action. Designated MVP and PRO player of the year.* Sport *magazine playoff MVP.* Many people rushed out to purchase season tickets to watch the midair antics and powerful slam dunks of Julius "Dr. J" Erving, who was far and away the best player on the team. So when franchise owner Roy Boe sold the rights to Dr. J to the Philadelphia 76ers for $3 million on October 20, just 24 hours before the official start of the season but well after season tickets had been sold, Nets fans were outraged. In a court case called Strauss v. Long Island Sports, Inc., a number of Nets season ticket holders sued the franchise and won their money back.

BACK TO JERSEY

BEFORE THE NEXT SEASON, BOE MOVED THE NETS back to their original state, and in September 1977, the New Jersey Nets were officially born. The team also acquired a new offensive star—rookie sensation Bernard King. That first year, the exciting young forward averaged 24 points and 9 rebounds a game. "What impresses me is how he shoots with such quickness and accuracy," said Red Holzman, a former New York Knicks coach. "Other teams overplay him and try to deny him the ball, but he keeps scoring."

During the Nets' first years in New Jersey, the nucleus of King, shot-blocking wizard George Johnson, and guard John Williamson kept the Nets near the middle of the NBA standings. As the Nets entered the 1980s, the team hired veteran NBA coach Larry Brown. Brown's first move was to select 21-year-old power forward Charles "Buck" Williams in the 1981 NBA Draft. A rugged rebounder and scorer,

Bernard King became a basketball legend on the playgrounds of New York before entering the NBA

Although most famous for his rim-shaking slam dunks, Darryl Dawkins was also a great rebounder

Williams was named the NBA Rookie of the Year. "Every team should be blessed with a Buck Williams," said former Nets star Rick Barry. "He's consistent, hardworking, and tough."

Coach Brown combined Buck Williams with a backcourt of Ray Williams and Otis Birdsong, center Darryl Dawkins, and sharpshooting forward Albert King (Bernard's younger brother) to create a well-balanced unit. The Nets rose among the NBA's elite teams with a 49–33 record in 1982–83. Everything was looking up until the last two weeks of the season, when Brown announced that he would be leaving the team. The announcement seemed to deflate the young Nets, who quickly shuffled out of the playoffs.

The following year, New Jersey added talented point guard Micheal Ray Richardson, and the Nets pulled off a major upset by eliminating Julius Erving's Philadelphia 76ers, the defending NBA champions, in an exciting first-round matchup in the 1984 playoffs. After two more winning seasons, the club went on an extended drought for the rest of the 1980s, reaching its low point with a franchise-worst 17–65 record in 1989–90.

DEATH OF A PIONEER

An influx of European players breathed new life into the NBA in the late 1980s and early '90s. Among those players was Drazen Petrovic, a native of Croatia who helped his national team win the Olympic silver medal in 1992. His enthusiasm for the game and sound outside and free-throw shooting skills impressed NBA fans, coaches, and players alike. Sadly, Petrovic's life was cut short. On a visit to see his girlfriend, a car in which he was a passenger smashed into a tractor-trailer on Germany's Autobahn roadway, killing him instantly. He was only 28 years old. Said NBA commissioner David Stern: "I know that a lasting part of his athletic legacy will be that he paved the way for other international players to compete successfully in the NBA."

THE NETS' TURNAROUND IN THE EARLY 1990S WAS

fueled by two top draft picks: power forward Derrick

Coleman and point guard Kenny Anderson. When he

was motivated, Coleman could dominate games, hitting

18-foot jumpers with deadly accuracy or making daring

moves inside. Anderson was an outstanding passer, but,

like Coleman, he was inconsistent and had a tendency

to commit too many turnovers.

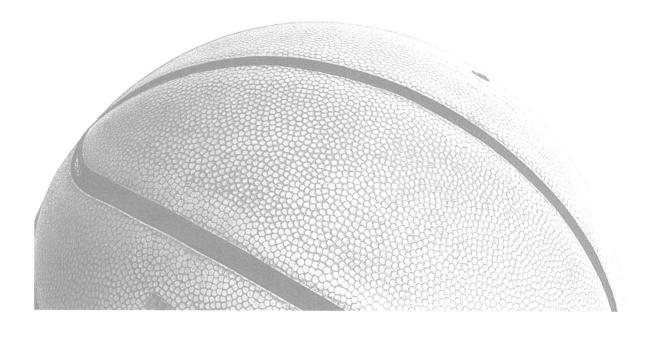

Quick point guard Kenny Anderson sparked the Nets' offensive attack for five seasons in the 1990s

22

Forward Keith Van Horn enjoyed his finest NBA season in 1999-00, averaging nearly 22 points a game

This talented duo, along with long-range bomber Drazen Petrovic from Croatia, powered the Nets to a 43–39 record in 1992–93, ending a seven-year streak of losing seasons. Then, in the summer of 1993, Petrovic was tragically killed in a car crash. The heartsick Nets finished 45–37 in 1993–94 but lost to the New York Knicks in the first round of the playoffs. "It's hard for you to imagine here in America, because you have so many great players," Drazen's brother, Aleksander Petrovic, said. "But we are a country of four million. Without him, basketball [in Croatia] takes three steps back."

Beset by injuries the next year, the Nets fell to a losing record again, and the team's management decided to clean house. Coleman and Anderson were traded, and new players such as swingman Kendall Gill and power forward Jayson Williams were brought in. But even successful college coach John Calipari could not turn the Nets' fortunes around.

The Nets picked early in several consecutive NBA Drafts in the late '90s, adding such talented newcomers as guard Kerry Kittles and forward Keith Van Horn. In a 1999 trade, the Nets acquired point guard Stephon Marbury, and former Los Angeles Lakers guard Byron Scott took over as the Nets' coach before the 2000–01 season.

JAYSON WILLIAMS, FALLEN STAR

Jayson Williams, a hard-nosed, 6-foot-10 forward, played six seasons for the Nets (1993–94 to 1998–99) and became an All-Star, a fan favorite, and a TV analyst following his playing career. But in February 2002, Williams fired a gun that killed his limousine driver. A jury convicted Williams of attempting to cover up the shooting but ruled the death accidental. Still, the reputation of Williams—once known for his charitable donations to AIDS victims (two of Williams's sisters died of AIDS)—had been tarnished. "When I'm retired, I want people to say, 'That's a good man,'" Williams wrote in his autobiography. "Even the ones who say, 'Isn't that the guy who used to be so wild, who used to be drinking and fighting so much, who was always getting in trouble?'"

24

Skinny but strong guard Kerry Kittles could score when needed but was best known for his tight defense

NETS TRADES

Trades in the NBA are a way of life, but it long seemed to Nets fans that they were getting the raw end of the deal too often. In 2001, however, New Jersey traded for All-Star point guard Jason Kidd, subsequently earning trips to the NBA Finals in 2002 and 2003. Then, just as it seemed the Nets were poised to trade Kidd in 2004–05, they didn't. Instead, they traded for high-flying guard Vince Carter, who took his game to a new level. "We've maybe let some things slip through the cracks," Kidd said of the Nets, who traded stars Kenyon Martin and Kerry Kittles in 2004 to save money and notoriously "traded" away Dr. J (for money) in 1976. "But [management is] in it to win. You could see that with this move."

FRESH NETS

IN THE 2000 NBA DRAFT, THE NETS SELECTED forward Kenyon Martin of the University of Cincinnati with the top overall pick. Martin loved to battle under the boards for rebounds and emphasized defense before offense. To prove the point, Martin chose six as his uniform number in honor of Bill Russell, one of the best defenders in NBA history. Still, the Nets struggled to a 26–56 record in 2000–01.

27

Despite standing only 6-foot-9, Kenyon Martin quickly became one of the NBA's premiere shot blockers

With his array of jaw-dropping moves and soaring dunks, Vince Carter reminded fans of the great Dr. J

The Nets made two key moves in 2001. First, they pulled off a draft-day deal for athletic forward Richard Jefferson out of the University of Arizona. Then they traded their failed experiment at point guard, Marbury, to Phoenix for All-Star point guard Jason Kidd, a magician with the ball. Said Nets president Rod Thorn, "Jason brought to us all of the things that go into making a basketball team a good team…but I think more than anything else, Jason brought a winning attitude."

The moves paid off immediately, and New Jersey pulled off a 26-game turnaround, going 52–30 and making it all the way to the 2002 NBA Finals. Although they were beaten by the Lakers, Kidd, Martin, Jefferson, and company charged back into the Finals again the next year. This time their opponent was the San Antonio Spurs, but the result was the same—a Finals loss.

After coming up short of the Finals the next year under new coach Lawrence Frank, the Nets looked to some new talent. In 2004–05, the Nets' 7-foot rookie center Nenad Krstic enjoyed a fine year, and the squad was bolstered by a midseason trade that brought in Vince Carter, an All-Star guard formerly with the Toronto Raptors. Carter's Dr. J-like athleticism meshed well with Kidd's great passing, and New Jersey improved quickly.

With the Nets seemingly ready for a renewed run at NBA glory, many New Jersey fans see shades of Dr. J flying through the air when they look at Vince Carter floating high to catch a lob pass from Jason Kidd today. It's a comforting sight, and one that the Nets hope triggers their own visions of that elusive first NBA championship trophy.

COACH FRANK

When the Nets promoted 33-year-old assistant coach Lawrence Frank to interim head coach in 2004, many fans, players, and basketball experts were astounded. Frank was younger than many NBA players, and with his floppy red hair, boyish appearance, and short stature, he did not look the part of an NBA head coach. But Frank seized the opportunity and held on tight, guiding the Nets to wins in his first 13 games as head coach (an NBA record) and landing a multi-year contract. All this from a man whose college basketball experience consisted of being the student manager while attending Indiana University. "I have become a tremendous fan," said Nets president Rod Thorn of Frank. "No one knows more, prepares better, or has as much passion for the game of basketball as Lawrence."

Perhaps the finest passer in the league, Jason Kidd helped take the Nets to two NBA Finals appearances